CHOOSE
MORE JOY!

So, how can YOU get happier? The most important step you can take on your journey to find more happiness is actually pretty easy; you need to make a conscious decision to be happier.

It's really that simple! If you don't welcome happiness into your life, you won't be able to fully recognise the joy you feel. And you'll probably only feel happy every now and then.

However, if you accept you're in control of your feelings and deserve to be happy every day, you can start feeling happier almost immediately!

How you choose to see things and behave shapes your world. If you decide to be gloomy, the chances are the world will seem pretty gloomy. Decide to be happy and your world will seem like a much happier place.

Your first step towards more happiness is a simple choice: do you want to be happier or are you OK with things as they are? The choice is yours.

DECIDE YOU ARE READY TO BE HAPPIER!

Find your path.

HOW TO BE UNICORN HAPPY

SIMPLE STEPS TO HELP BOOST YOUR HAPPINESS!

instagram.com/unicornhappinessbook
instagram.com/youareaunicornbook

Visit my website, vincentx2.com to find
out more about my books.

This book is dedicated to all the amazing
unicorns in my life, especially Tom.

HEY THERE!

Welcome to *How To Be Unicorn Happy*. I decided to write this book after the amazing response my creative journal, *You Are A Unicorn*, received when it was published in April, 2017.

Inspired by the *You Are A Unicorn* Instagram page (please follow @YouAreAUnicornBook), I wanted to share my positivity with as many people as possible, and thought this book could be a good way to achieve that.

I really hope you enjoy *How To Be Unicorn Happy*. It's filled with beautiful pictures and tons of inspirational ways for you to welcome more positivity and happiness into your life – and live every day like a unicorn!

IT'S TIME FOR MORE HAPPINESS!

Do you take your happiness for granted? That it's something that will simply slot into place when everything aligns correctly? I certainly did until recently. I thought it was something that would just happen if I was a 'good' person.

Don't get me wrong, I wasn't feeling particularly downbeat, but I wasn't in the best place either. I'd devoted three years to a project that hadn't panned out as well as I'd expected, and I was working through the loss of my father to cancer.

It's easy to take it for granted that we'll be happier 'one day'. But life can get in the way, and dealing with friends, family, work, relationships etc can be challenging.

Fortunately I came to the conclusion recently that feeling happy is a choice. Like most things of any value, happiness doesn't just come along and land in our laps. We have to work at it every day.

However, the first step we must take towards happinesss is to accept that we're happy right now.

YOU CREATE YOUR REALITY.

Not everything in our lives has to be OK. The chances are, there will always be something worrying going on in the world. But if we choose to be happy today, right now, no matter what's going on, no one can take it away from us.

Last January, I decided to work out what makes me feel happiest; what I could do every day that would bring me joy. Once I started working at being happier, my mood lifted, I felt energised and started exploring an exciting new direction.

It didn't take me long to see creativity was a key factor in my happiness. With a background in children's publishing, I've spent most of my career interviewing people, and writing about everything from wildlife and science, to movies and TV shows. I was even an agony uncle for 10 years!

I knew that I wanted to do more creative work, and use it to help other people get in touch with their positivity and creativity. This realisation eventually lead to the release of my book, *You Are A Unicorn* – a fun journal to help release creativity and boost positivity. *How To Be Unicorn Happy* is a natural progression, with lots of ways to help you welcome more happiness into your life, including inspirational quotes and pictures.

I can't guarantee all of the techniques in this book will work for you – you might need to try a different approach for some things – but I promise once you start working at being happier, it's only a matter of time before you are!

FALL IN LOVE
WITH MOMENTS!

SAY IT LOUD!

Once you've decided to be happier – and I'm guessing you have, as you've read this far – it's important to acknowledge the decision and really commit to it. This gives your intention more power, and means you're more likely to stick with it.

A good way of doing this is to verbalise your thoughts. So find somewhere private and repeat each of these statements out loud, three times:

*I CHOOSE TO BE HAPPY

*I DESERVE TO BE HAPPY

* I AM HAPPY IN THIS MOMENT

DON'T GIVE UP.

TIME TO JOURNAL!

Now you've decided you want to be happier – and are ready to really work at it – what's the best way to get started?

A great way to kickstart your happiness is to take up journaling. Keeping a journal is a powerful tool – it can really help you engage with your thoughts!

Starting a journal was one of the first steps I took on my happiness journey. I started my first journal back in 2005. It was basically a list of doodles and ideas that made me smile. More recently, I've used journaling to help me work out where I am in my life, where I want to go, and what kind of person I want to be.

Getting clarity can be hard sometimes, and I found journaling was a great way to focus my mind. I was already on the right path, but journaling helped me explore new ideas and options, and work out what direction to take. Keeping a journal was also fun, and made me feel more optimistic and excited about the future!

You can use anything for your journal – a notebook, tablet or something designed for journaling. I have a range of Happy Unicorn notebooks on Amazon that would be perfect!

CHOOSE
HAPPINESS

Ready to start journaling? Great! Now decide what you're going to write in – this will be your special Happiness Journal!

It's important to write in your journal regularly. I recommend writing in yours every day for around 20 minutes. Try to make journaling part of your daily routine – it's a good way to commit to being more happy. Don't stress if you miss a day though as that would be counter-productive!

KEEPING A JOURNAL CAN...

- Improve your IQ and memory
- Make you feel more positive
- Help you achieve goals
- Increase your creativity
- Strengthen your self-discipline
- Reduce your stress levels
- Boost your self-confidence
- Leave you feeling like a unicorn!

One of the great things about journaling is that it doesn't have to be perfect. Writing in your journal is a release. So don't worry if you make a spelling mistake or a page ends up looking messy.

If you find it hard to get started on your journaling journey, check out my *Unicorn Happiness Journal* – available on Amazon. With prompts on each page, it'll have you journaling in no time!

10 JOURNALING TIPS

1. WRITE WHATEVER FEELS RIGHT!

2. ALWAYS KEEP A PEN AND PAPER HANDY!

3. BEGIN ANYWHERE – FORGET ABOUT SPELLING AND PUNCTUATION!

4. WRITE IN A PLACE THAT'S RELAXING AND CALM!

5. LOOK FORWARD TO YOUR JOURNALING TIME!

6. DOODLE IF YOU FEEL LIKE IT!

7. BE HONEST – DON'T CENSOR YOURSELF!

8. JOURNALING IS 'YOU TIME' – ENJOY IT!

9. YOUR JOURNAL IS PRIVATE – SHARE PAGES IF YOU WANT TO THOUGH!

10. REMEMBER –THERE ARE NO RULES!

Start
where
you are.

"KEEP A NOTEBOOK. TRAVEL WITH IT, EAT WITH IT, SLEEP WITH IT. PAPER IS LESS PERISHABLE THAN GREY MATTER."

JACK LONDON

"KEEPING A JOURNAL IS HAVING A RELATIONSHIP WITH YOUR MIND."

NATALIE GOLDBERG

"JOURNAL WRITING IS A VOYAGE TO THE INTERIOR."

CHRISTINA BALDWIN

Expect miracles!

Focus on feelings!

If you want to feel happier, it's really important to register how you're feeling throughout each day.

This can help reveal the things that leave you feeling fantastic, and highlight any blockages you might have to feeling happier.

One way to focus on your emotions is to try and keep an eye on them, and consciously recognise the feelings you're experiencing. However, this isn't always easy to do – especially if you're having a stressful day! I've used the following technique for years and have found it's a really effective way to tune into feelings.

AS WITH ALL OF THE ACTIVITIES IN THIS BOOK, USE THE ONES THAT APPEAL TO YOU MOST. WE'RE ALL DIFFERENT, SO PICK AND CHOOSE THE ONES THAT ARE BEST FOR YOU!

Ready to focus on how you are feeling? This simple activity only takes around 10 minutes and all you need is a mirror, something to write in and a quiet place where you won't be disturbed.

Thoughts become things.

HAPPINESS EXERCISE 1

1. Find a quiet place and get comfortable. Using a mirror, look yourself in the eye and read each of these statements out loud.

2. Repeat each statement 10 times and as you speak, think about how the words are making you feel.

3. Do you feel worthy of feeling good? Are the words having a physical effect? Whatever you feel is fine – there's no right or wrong with this exercise.

* I LIKE MYSELF THE WAY I AM
* I HAVE NO REGRETS ABOUT THE PAST
* I LOVE BEING ME
* MY WORLD IS FULL OF OPPORTUNITIES
* I AM OPEN TO NEW IDEAS

This exercise helps you register your feelings. Try writing different statements and see how reading them out affects you.

You
become
what you
believe!

LOVE TO LIST!

Lists are a brilliant way of boosting positivity. Writing down all of the different ways you've felt good is a powerful reminder of the positive, happy things you might otherwise take for granted.

Once you start recognising more happiness in your life, you'll find it easier to notice happy feelings.

Grab a pen and take a few minutes to write a quick happiness list. Write down anything that has gone right recently or made you feel good. Here are a few things from my last list...

* HAD A REALLY GREAT LIE-IN
* TOP SHOPPING & LUNCH WITH TOM
* COOKED AN AWESOME CURRY
* MET PHIL & JON'S PUPPY, NELSON
* DELICIOUS BREAKFAST WITH DAN
* FUN CATCH-UP WITH JOSEPHINE
* GREAT PHONECALL WITH MICHELLE
* FINALLY COMPLETED MY CAT JIGSAW
* LOVELY DINNER WITH SANDIE & EMMA
* COOL TRIP TO SEE JOHAN & DAVE

Be kinder to yourself.

KINDNESS COUNTS

A great way to feel happier is to spread happiness. I'm a firm believer that a friendly smile or a kind word or gesture can really change the course of someone's day.

What we say and do, and the energy we project into the world, is enormously powerful. You can impact someone's life in many ways, so why not choose to be a positive influence?!

Showing compassion for others not only helps make them feel good, it boosts your mood too. Being kind produces the hormone oxytocin, which improves our frame of mind, lowers blood pressure, and increases our self-esteem and optimism.

It's easy to get caught up in our busy lives, but showing kindness really does count. Altruistic acts not only feel good, they have a domino effect. Studies have shown being kind is contagious. When you do a good deed for someone they're more likely be kind to someone else, as is anyone who witnessed your kindness!

Grab your Happiness Journal or a notebook and jot down 15 ways that you've been kind recently. Recognising your good deeds will boost your mood and encourage you to do more kind stuff!

Sing your own song.

10 RANDOM ACTS OF KINDNESS

Any act of kindness, no matter how big or small, can really make a difference. Try these suggestions and share some positivity...

1 STICK UP
Write positive phrases on sticky notes, then stick them anywhere that needs an injection of kindness.

2 OPEN SESAME
Hold the door open for someone – even if they aren't carrying stuff or pushing a baby buggy.

3 POST IT
It's easy to take social media for granted, but if someone posts something you enjoy, why not let them know? A quick comment will show you appreciate their time and effort.

4 WRITE ON
Show someone you care by taking the time to write them a handwritten note or letter. It takes longer than writing a text or email, but they'll love your personal gesture!

5 SHOWER POWER
Keep an extra umbrella somewhere handy in case someone needs to borrow it.

Be
here
now.

6 ALL CHANGE
Give a stranger a nice surprise by leaving some loose change by a vending machine. You could even put the money in a small bag, with a note that says "This treat's on me!"

7 GIFT IT
Buy or make a small gift for someone to lift their spirits and get them smiling. Cakes and cookies are great for this!

8 SPEAK UP
When you meet up with a friend, be sure to tell them if you like the jacket they're wearing or if their hair looks nice. Everyone feels great when they're paid a compliment!

9 DO MORE
If you're helping someone with something, go one better and try to do even more for them. They're sure to appreciate you making an extra special effort to help.

10 HELP OUT
Next time a friend asks if you need a hand, allow them to help. Showing kindness towards you will make them feel good – and it will mean your task gets done quicker too!

I'D LOVE TO HEAR ABOUT HOW YOU HAVE SHOWN KINDNESS. PLEASE MAIL YOUR STORIES TO KIND@VINCENTX2.COM THANK YOU!

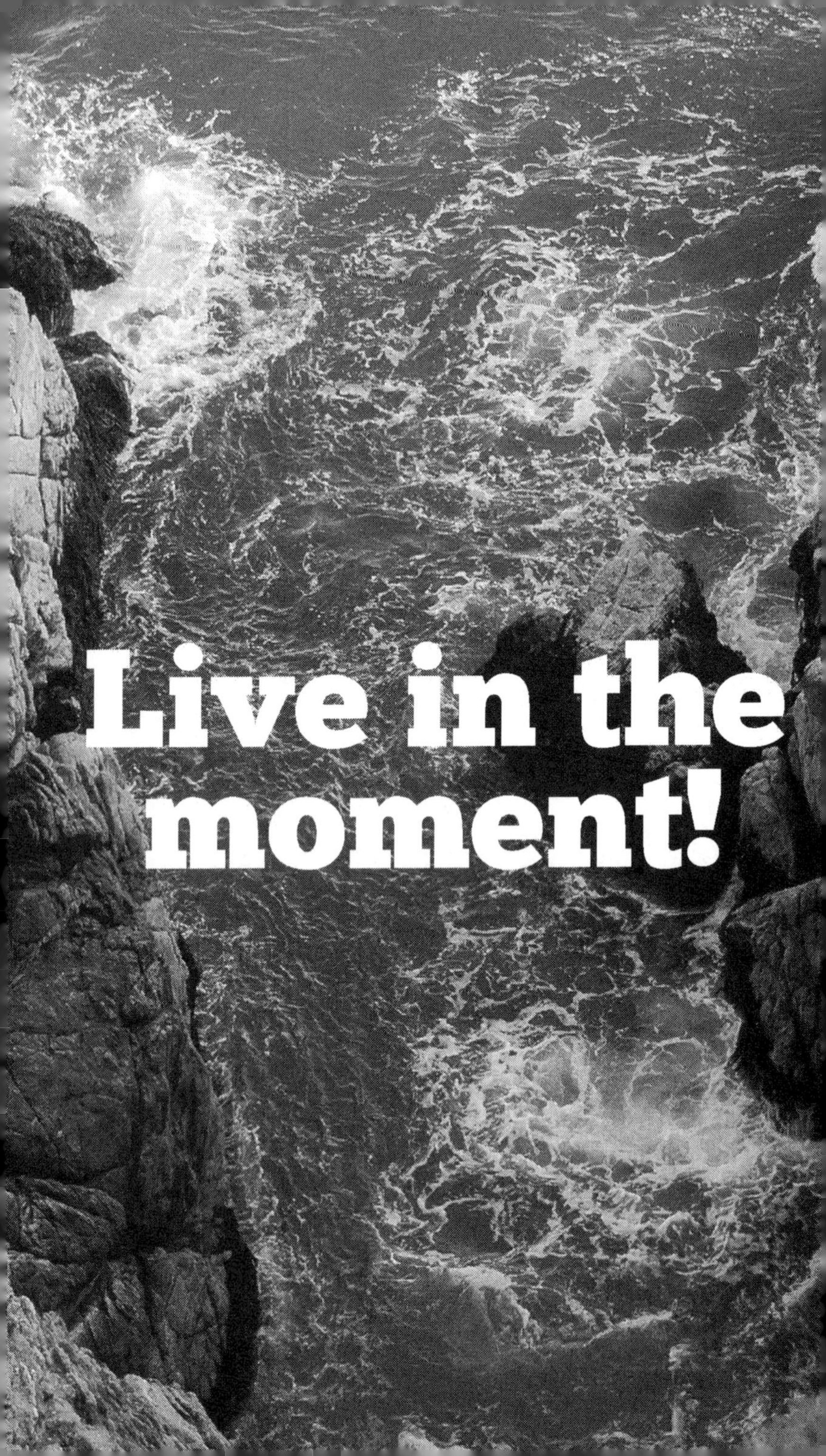
Live in the
moment!

"A SINGLE ACT OF KINDNESS THROWS OUT ROOTS IN ALL DIRECTIONS, AND THE ROOTS SPRING UP AND MAKE NEW TREES."

AMELIA EARHART

"THERE IS NO NEED FOR TEMPLES OR COMPLICATED PHILOSOPHIES. MY BRAIN AND MY HEART ARE MY TEMPLES; MY PHILOSOPHY IS KINDNESS."

DALAI LAMA

"KIND WORDS CAN BE EASY TO SPEAK BUT THEIR ECHOES ARE TRULY ENDLESS."

MOTHER TERESA

Radiate Love.

Forgive the past

If you're feeling unhappy and life doesn't seem to be flowing freely, it may well be because you are holding on to negative moments and memories.

Feeling angry or resentful about things that have happened blocks your potential for happiness. It's impossible to fill your life with positivity and joy if you're carrying negative baggage around with you. To feel truly happy in the present, you must let go of negativity from your past.

Maybe you feel hurt or angry about something that has happened? Or guilty and frustrated about the way a situation was handled? Whatever you're feeling might be completely justified, but wasting energy on negative emotions will only hold you back.

Blaming someone else for the past is holding on to something that can't be changed. You can't rewrite history, but you can try to come to terms with it and move forward.

The key to doing this is forgiveness. If you want to move on from a negative memory, make a conscious decision to forgive what has happened. This will set you free from the past and give you permission to embrace more happiness.

RELEASE YOUR INNER UMCORN!

Forgiveness doesn't mean you're accepting bad behaviour or letting it continue. Instead, it releases negative energy, and helps you deal with and resolve difficult situations.

A great way to truly forgive something is to use affirmations. These are repeated sentences that influence our conscious and subconscious mind.

I use affirmations every day and they definitely help make me feel more positive, confident and happy. Repeating phrases helps change the way we think, and influences our behaviour, habits, actions and reactions.

The affirmations on the next page will help you choose to release the past and create a happier, more fulfilled life!

THINK HAPPY THOUGHTS!

HAPPINESS EXERCISE 2

Repeat each of these affirmations 20 times every day until you feel you have moved on from the past...

* I AM PRESENT AND FORGIVE WHAT HAPPENED. I RELEASE THE PAST.

* I EMBRACE THIS MOMENT AND CREATE HOW I FEEL.

* I AM COMPLETELY FREE OF THE PAST. MY POTENTIAL IS LIMITLESS.

* MY PAST IS NOW HEALED AND I MOVE FORWARDS WITH LOVE.

TOP TIP

Affirmations work best when they're done every day and repeated often. Try writing affirmations on some card and keeping it with your phone or in your coat pocket. The card will remind you to say the positive phrases!

Do more
of what
makes you

happy!

BE PRESENT!

A simple way to embrace positivity and increase the joy in your life is to recognise each moment and really connect with it. Right now is the only time zone that really exists. The past has passed and the future hasn't arrived yet. So engaging more with life as it happens – and being more mindful – will mean you get much more out of it!

Life can seem so fast and hectic these days, but how you see things is up to you. Once you work at being more present, it'll seem like you have more time and that life has more feel-good opportunities!

NOTICE EACH moment.

Right now
is all that
matters.

"THERE ARE ONLY TWO WAYS TO LIVE LIFE.
AS THOUGH NOTHING IS A MIRACLE OR
AS THOUGH EVERYTHING IS A MIRACLE."

ALBERT EINSTEIN

"THE LITTLE THINGS? THE LITTLE
MOMENTS? THEY AREN'T LITTLE."

JON KABAT-ZINN

"THE ONLY WAY TO LIVE IS BY
ACCEPTING EACH MINUTE AS
AN UNREPEATABLE MIRACLE."

TARA BRACH

Love every
MINUTE.

feel right now!

Whatever you're doing, from mundane everyday chores to enjoying special occasions and new opportunities, living in the moment will soon have you feeling happier. The more you focus on being present, the more you'll notice things that make you happy!

Here are some handy ways to help you focus on being right here, right now:

DO ONE THING AT A TIME

Forget multi-tasking. If you're eating, just eat. If you're talking, don't check your phone for new texts. Focussing on doing one thing at a time helps you fully experience it – and enjoy it more!

SLOW DOWN

Try not to rush things. Take your time and be deliberate. The more attention you pay, the more enjoyable things will be!

Make the most of now!

LET GO AND DO LESS
Next time you find yourself filling your day with tasks, make a list and work out which ones are really important. Then cross off the tasks that can wait. Rushing from one thing to the next will distract you from the present. Let go of unimportant stuff and concentrate on the things that matter.

TAKE A BREAK
Even on your busiest day, try to find at least five minutes to relax somewhere quiet and do nothing. Sit in silence and become aware of your breathing. Let thoughts float in and out of your mind. Notice the space around you and find peace in the stillness.

DON'T WORRY
Watch out for any worries you might have about the future. Whenever you catch yourself fretting about what might happen, practise bringing yourself back into the present. Focus on what you're doing and remind yourself that you're OK.

TUNE IN
Whatever you're doing, slow down and savour the experience. Tune in to each moment and focus on each action. You'll enjoy everything more!

TOP TIP
Being mindful isn't always easy. If you're finding it hard to focus on the present, stick with it and keep practising. You'll soon feel the benefits – and get a happiness boost!

You are in
charge of
your destiny.

"MINDFULNESS IS RECEIVING THE PRESENT MOMENT, PLEASANT OR UNPLEASANT, JUST AS IT IS, WITHOUT EITHER CLINGING TO IT OR REJECTING IT."

SYLVIA BOORSTEIN

"DO NOT DWELL IN THE PAST, DO NOT DREAM OF THE FUTURE, CONCENTRATE THE MIND ON THE PRESENT MOMENT."

BUDDHA

"WHEN YOU REALIZE NOTHING IS LACKING, THE WHOLE WORLD BELONGS TO YOU."

LAO TZU

15 HAPPINESS HABITS

Here are 15 ways to work more positivity into your day. Give each one a go and see which suggestions work best for you!

1 BE GRATEFUL FOR WHAT YOU HAVE

2 LEND A HAND AND HELP OTHERS

3 SURROUND YOURSELF WITH POSITIVE, FUN, SUPPORTIVE PEOPLE!

4 WAKE UP EARLY! IT'S ENERGISING TO BE AWAKE BEFORE ANYONE ELSE!

5 LISTEN TO YOUR FEELINGS

6 TRY TO LOOK ON THE BRIGHT SIDE!

7 ACCEPT THINGS THAT CAN'T BE CHANGED

8 EXERCISE – IT'S GOOD FOR YOU PHYSICALLY AND MENTALLY!

9 RELAX AT THE END OF THE DAY!

10 LEARN NEW SKILLS AND TRY DIFFERENT THINGS!

Be thankful
for what
you have.

11 TRY TO SEE PROBLEMS AS CHALLENGES.

12 DON'T COMPARE YOURSELF TO OTHERS – LOVE YOUR INDIVIDUALITY!

13 DREAM BIG! THERE'S NO LIMIT TO WHAT YOU CAN ACHIEVE!

14 FOCUS YOUR MIND WITH DAILY MEDITATION.

15 BE HONEST WITH EVERYONE, INCLUDING YOURSELF.

BE THANKFUL

Focussing on what we're grateful for is a quick and easy reminder that life is good. Thankful people are less stressed, more positive and feel more capable of reaching their goals.

A great way to harness this is to keep a gratitude journal. This is a book where you write down what you're grateful for each day. Anything and everything good in your life can be listed, no matter how small. I've been keeping a gratitude journal for a year now, and love filling it in – it's a wonderful reminder of how lucky I am! If you'd rather just keep one journal, I'd really recommend including a gratitude section in your Happiness Journal.

YOUR WORLD IS A SAFE PLACE.

HAPPINESS EXERCISE 3

This exercise will help you focus on the good things in your life, and highlight stuff you don't need anymore.

* GRAB A PEN AND PAPER

* DRAW TWO LARGE SQUARES

* LABEL SQUARE 1: 'THANKS!'

* LABEL SQUARE 2: 'NO THANKS!'

* FILL SQUARE 1 WITH THINGS YOU ARE GRATEFUL FOR...

* FILL THE OTHER SQUARE WITH THINGS YOU DON'T WANT IN YOUR LIFE...

DRAW MORE SQUARES IF YOU NEED MORE ROOM!

Reminding ourselves of all the positive stuff in our lives is a great leveller. Also, identifying situations that aren't making us happy is our first step in dealing with them.

Focus on the good.

"BE THANKFUL FOR WHAT YOU HAVE;
YOU'LL END UP HAVING MORE. CONCENTRATE
ON WHAT YOU DON'T HAVE, AND YOU WILL
NEVER, EVER HAVE ENOUGH."

OPRAH WINFREY

"ACKNOWLEDGING THE GOOD YOU ALREADY
HAVE IN YOUR LIFE IS THE FOUNDATION
FOR ALL ABUNDANCE."

ECKHART TOLLE

"GRATITUDE HELPS YOU TO GROW AND EXPAND;
IT BRINGS JOY AND LAUGHTER INTO YOUR
LIFE AND THE LIVES OF THOSE AROUND YOU."

EILEEN CADDY

OWN YOUR CHOICES.

HAPPINESS EXERCISE 4

This simple visualisation will help you harness the positive power of gratitude.

1. Find a quiet place somewhere you won't be disturbed. Then sit or lay down and become aware of your breathing.

2. Next, close your eyes and focus on your body. How does it feel? Relax any parts that are holding tension.

3. Breathe slowly and deeply, and notice your body relax more with each breath.

4. Now picture yourself standing in an empty warehouse. Slowly start to fill it with the stuff in your life that you're grateful for.

5. Picture people you're happy to know, and experiences you are thankful to have had. Visualise anything that's improved your life.

6. How does it feel to be in your warehouse once it's full? Notice the feeling and enjoy it.

7. When you're ready, become aware of the room around you and open your eyes.

Focus on what
makes you happy.

Banish bad days!

Next time you're having a 'bad day' ask yourself why it's so bad. Maybe you got up late, then spilled coffee everywhere. Or perhaps you lost your door keys and ended up missing an important appointment. Whatever stuff contributed to your 'bad day', the chances are it's all in the past – but you can't help thinking about it, which just makes you more fed up, and your 'bad day' even worse. We've all been there – it's a really easy pattern to fall into.

This is because negative situations heighten your emotions and trigger your survival instinct. This narrows your mind and focusses your thoughts on trying to solve the problematic situation.

Thinking negative thoughts like "I'm so clumsy, I can't do anything right" or "What a disaster, I'm never going to get to this appointment in time," programs your brain to block everything else out so you're free to tackle the negativity. Unfortunately, thinking this way also prevents your brain from seeing the other options and choices that are available, meaning your negative thoughts spiral and make you feel worse.

Luckily, there are ways you can turn 'bad days' around – and the key is focussing on positivity!

APPRECIATE WHERE
YOU ARE RIGHT NOW.

If you find yourself having a 'bad day', redirect negative thoughts by focussing on positive emotions like joy and contentment. Something 'bad' might happen but focussing on positive areas of your life will help put things into perspective, and let you see the bigger picture.

Here are some ways you can use positivity to bring happiness back into a difficult day...

POSITIVITY POWER!

• Carry a picture of someone you love and respect around with you. Look at the image and remember why you admire the person when you need a positivity boost.

• Write down three reasons you're lucky on a sticky note and keep it in your purse or wallet. Then use your lucky list to remind yourself of the positive stuff in your life.

• Close your eyes, breathe slowly, and visualise yourself at a time when you felt safe and secure. Recall how you felt and let the positive feelings wash over you.

• Grab your journal and write a story about a positive experience you've had.

Embrace your destiny.

HAPPINESS EXERCISE 5

Repeat these affirmations 20 times every day to welcome more positivity into your life...

* I AM HONEST WITH MYSELF. I ACCEPT WHAT I CAN'T CHANGE AND MOVE ON.

* I HAVE UNLIMITED POTENTIAL. I AM ALWAYS EXPANDING AND EVOLVING.

* I RADIATE LOVE, JOY AND GRATITUDE.

* I NOW TAKE RESPONSIBILITY FOR MY OWN HAPPINESS. I AM IN CONTROL!

* I RELEASE ALL NEGATIVITY FROM MY LIFE. I FOCUS ON BEING POSITIVE AND PRODUCTIVE!

"OPTIMISM IS THE FAITH THAT LEADS TO ACHIEVEMENT."

HELEN KELLER

"YOU POSSESS THE KEYS TO YOUR BEING. YOU CARRY THE PASSPORT TO YOUR OWN HAPPINESS."

DIANE VON FURSTENBERG

"WE DON'T SEE THINGS AS THEY ARE, WE SEE THEM AS WE ARE."

ANAIS NIN

OWN WHO
YOU ARE.

ACCEPT YOUSELF!

Another step you must take on the path to true happiness is self-acceptance. This might sound simplistic, but *really* accepting yourself isn't always as easy as it sounds.

Don't make the same mistake I did and think that because you have OK self-esteem, you must also have OK self-acceptance. Self-esteem and self-acceptance are sometimes confused, and although they're related, they aren't the same. Self-esteem refers to how valuable or worthwhile we see ourselves. Self-acceptance is more unconditional and involves embracing ourselves completely – not just the positive stuff, but our weaknesses, limitations and quirks.

To feel totally happy, it's important to look at the parts of yourself you're not always comfortable with, and try and accept them anyway. You might not like some of your character traits, but they're still part of you – and contribute to what makes you such a special person!

The more self-acceptance you have, the more happiness you'll allow yourself to receive. So give yourself a break and work at truly accepting who you are. You're the only you that has ever existed and you are amazing!

You can't fail at being yourself.

I've found these self-acceptance techniques really useful. Don't feel you need to start doing all of them at once. Give one or two a go and see if they help, then try a few more until you find which techniques work best for you!

NOTICE YOUR THOUGHTS

Close your eyes and let thoughts and feelings come and go as you focus on your breathing. Let your thoughts wash over you and just observe them. Practise this for a few minutes every day.

ACKNOWLEDGE EVERYTHING

As you notice your thoughts (whether they're happy, sad, negative or positive) try to acknowledge and accept them. We often want to make negatives into positives, but instead of denying a negative feeling, let it linger and accept that it's there. Your feelings are part of you and they are all OK. Feelings are opportunities to learn about yourself. So instead of running away from a negative thought, try to embrace it and look for the chance to learn from it.

STOP JUDGING YOURSELF

Once you start paying more attention to your thoughts, you might notice you rate yourself as you go through the day – judging how good you are at things and comparing yourself to others. Whenever you find yourself doing this, question why it's happening and what you're getting from it. It'll soon become clear that it's not a useful habit and you'll be able to stop doing it.

LOVE BEING YOU

Before you get up each morning, think of five things you love about yourself. If something challenging has happened recently, ask yourself what you learnt from the experience. If you think of a trait that you're not happy with, try to work out how you can be grateful for it anyway.

LOOK FOR THE LESSON

It's easy to see successes as good and failures as bad, but something can be learned from every experience – even the unsuccessful things can teach us something about ourselves. Try to look for the lesson in every situation.

OBSERVE NEGATIVITY

Next time you catch yourself being negative, step back and observe your emotions. When did you start feeling like this? And what's making you feel this way? The negative feelings aren't part of you and they will pass, so try to learn from them and prepare to move on.

TALK IT OUT

Sometimes it can be easy to get lost in our own thoughts. If this happens, try talking things through with a person you trust. It can really help clarify your feelings.

TOP TIP

List challenges you've faced. Then think of positive ways you've grown from each situation – the lessons you've learnt, connections you've made etc. The past has no power over you but it has helped you grow!

HAPPINESS EXERCISE 6

This simple guided meditation will help boost your self-esteem.

1. Sit or lay down in a quiet place where you won't be disturbed, and become aware of your breathing.

2. Close your eyes and feel your whole body start to unwind.

3. Breathe slowly and deeply, feeling your body relax more with each breath.

4. Now think about something you're proud of – a skill, talent, or something you have said or done that makes you feel good.

5. Feel the sense of pride grow in your heart and expand with every breath.

6. Know that you deserve to feel proud of your achievements and that they encourage you to accomplish more great things.

7. Enjoy this feeling of pride for as long as you like. Remember how it feels if you ever question your abilities. You can do anything!

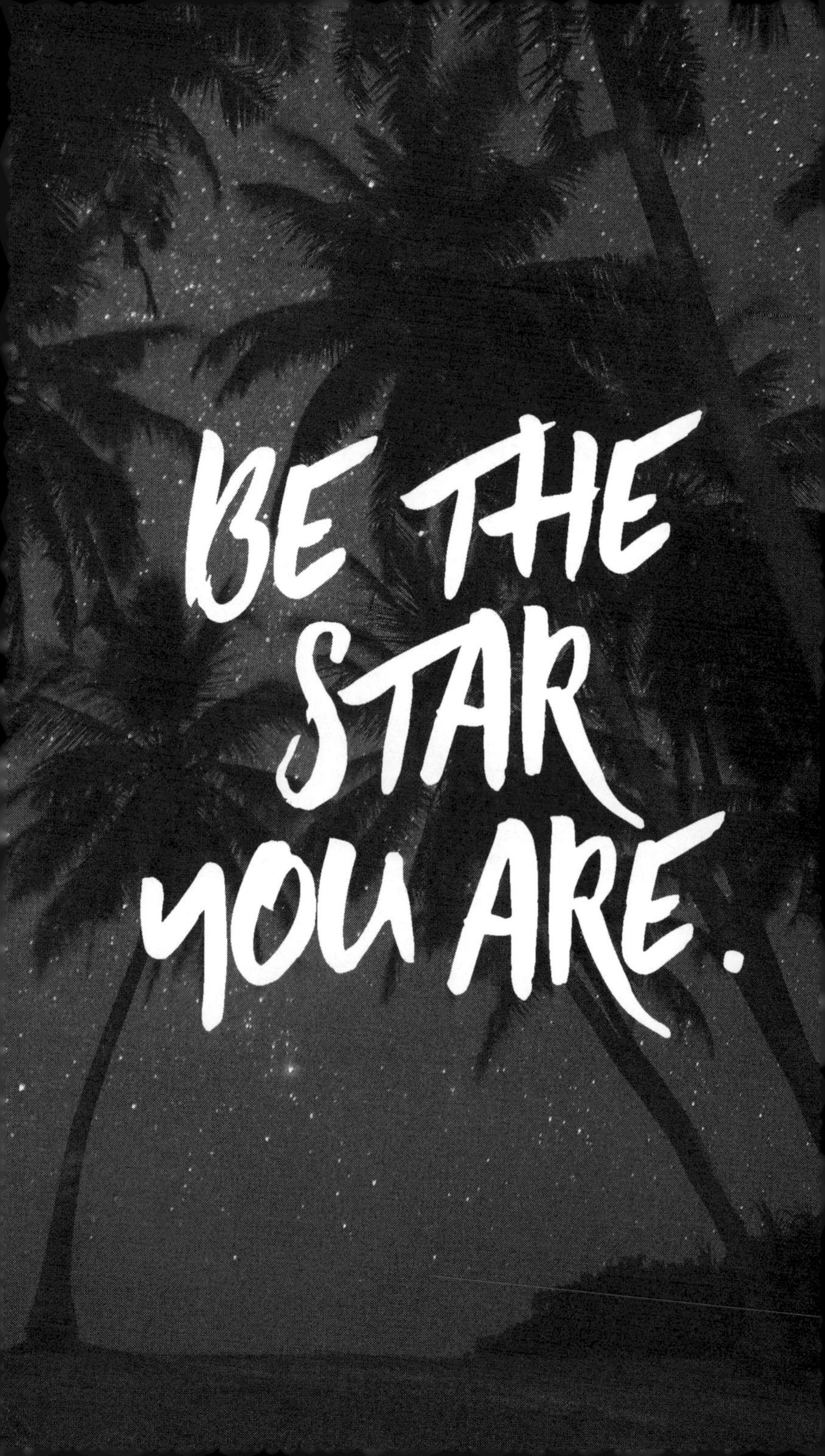
BE THE
STAR
YOU ARE.

"THERE IS SOMETHING WONDERFULLY BOLD AND LIBERATING ABOUT SAYING YES TO OUR ENTIRE IMPERFECT AND MESSY LIFE."

TARA BRACH

"TO BE BEAUTIFUL MEANS TO BE YOURSELF. YOU DON'T NEED TO BE ACCEPTED BY OTHERS. YOU NEED TO ACCEPT YOURSELF."

THICH NHAT HANH

"EVERY EXPERIENCE, NO MATTER HOW BAD IT SEEMS, HOLDS WITHIN IT A BLESSING OF SOME KIND. THE GOAL IS TO FIND IT."

BUDDHA

Create
yourself
every day.

set goals!

Whether they're career objectives, relationship aims or smaller things you want to accomplish on a daily basis, achieving goals is an essential part of living a happy and healthy life.

Research has shown that aiming to help others leads to more happiness in the long run, so make sure you set goals that benefit other people as well as yourself. Helping others strengthens our bond with the world and helps us build more meaningful relationships. So it's no wonder it leaves us feeling great!

These are good questions to ask when you set yourself new goals:

* WHAT DO I WANT TO ACHIEVE?
* WHO WILL I BE HELPING?
* HOW LONG WILL IT TAKE?
* HOW CHALLENGING WILL I FIND IT?
* WHAT STEPS MUST I TAKE TO SUCCEED?

FOCUS ON WHAT
COULD GO RIGHT.

A great way to get started with new goals is to think about past achievements. How did they make you feel? Would you like to do something similar? Or maybe you want to try something completely different?

Grab a notebook – or your Happiness Journal – and make a list of your proudest accomplishments. It can be a really long list or you can start off with a few things and add to it whenever something new occurs to you. This list will help remind you of the amazing things you are capable of, no matter how big or small!

MAKE IT HAPPEN!

Set motivational goals. Ask why each objective's important to you. Once you identify the value in achieving something, you're more likely to see it through.

Be specific. The more clear and well-defined a goal is, the easier it will be to achieve.

Be realistic. Setting goals you have no hope of achieving will only leave you feeling demotivated.

Give yourself a deadline. It will increase your sense of urgency and you'll complete your task quicker!

"THE ONLY LIMIT TO THE HEIGHT OF YOUR ACHIEVEMENTS IS THE REACH OF YOUR DREAMS AND YOUR WILLINGNESS TO WORK FOR THEM."

MICHELLE OBAMA

"IF YOU WANT TO BE HAPPY, SET A GOAL THAT COMMANDS YOUR THOUGHTS, LIBERATES YOUR ENERGY AND INSPIRES YOUR HOPES."

ANDREW CARNEGIE

"GOALS ARE DREAMS WITH DEADLINES."

DIANA SCHARF

Everything will be OK.

DREAM ON!

Another way I like to focus on positivity and happiness is by using a dream board. These are also known as 'vision boards' but I prefer 'dream board' as I think it sounds more magical!

A dream board is a collection of images, quotes and inspirational stuff, that's grouped together and displayed on a board. It's a great way to call attention to the things you want to achieve. Plus, dream boards are really fun to put together!

The secret to creating an effective dream board is focussing on how you want it to *feel*. If you can connect with it emotionally, your board will be much more powerful, and really bring your hopes and dreams to life!

Before you start making your dream board, take a moment to think about your life and what you'd like to achieve. Make a note of the things you want to change and the areas you'd like to develop.

Some people make separate boards for the different areas of their life. I prefer to just have one board that covers everything. As with the rest of this book, do what feels right and create as many dream boards as you want!

PLACE YOUR DREAM BOARD SOMEWHERE YOU'LL NOTICE IT OFTEN. THAT WAY, YOU'LL VISUALISE YOUR GOALS BEING SUCCESSFUL EACH TIME YOU SEE IT!

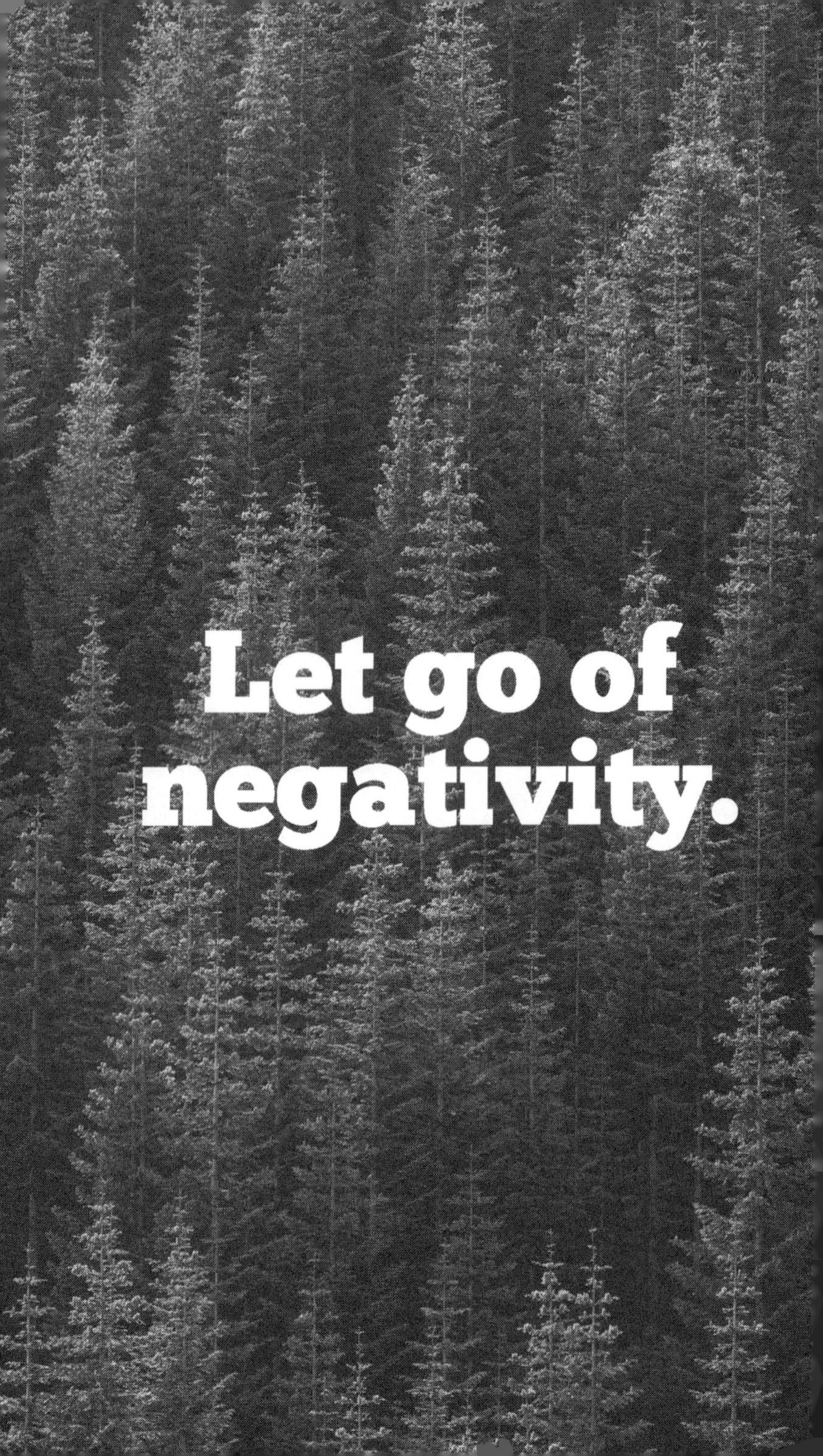
Let go of negativity.

HAPPINESS EXERCISE 7

Follow these simple steps to make your own motivational dream board!

WHAT YOU'LL NEED

- A pin board or cork board
- Scissors
- Tape, a glue stick or pins
- Magazines and photos
- Doodles, notes and mementos

UPDATE YOUR DREAM BOARD WHENEVER IT FEELS RIGHT. I REVISIT MINE IN JANUARY, SO I CAN BEGIN THE NEW YEAR WITH A FRESH START!

1. Choose a time to put your dream board together when you won't be disturbed.

2. First, work out what you're going to put on your board. Don't worry about making it perfect, you can always change things as you go along.

3. Next, lay everything out and decide where it's going to go on the dream board. Leave space in between each item, or let things overlap – it's up to you!

4. Now start gluing and pinning stuff to your board, filling it with things that represent your dreams. Let rip and see what happens. It's your dream board and anything goes!

FEEL-GOOD FRIENDS

Having a successful social life can be the difference between feeling happy and feeling *very* happy.

Knowing you have a circle of friends who love and support you isn't just reassuring, it can boost your confidence and raise your self-esteem. So investing time, energy and attention in your most important relationships is a surefire way to increase the good feelings in your life.

Finding friends who accept you and believe in you isn't always easy. A good way to establish a rock solid support system is to look at your friendship circle and ask these questions...

* WHO MAKES ME LAUGH?

* WHO SPEAKS NEGATIVELY TO ME?

* WHO HURTS MY FEELINGS?

* WHO ENCOURAGES ME?

* WHY AM I FRIENDS WITH THIS PERSON?

DISTANCE YOURSELF FROM ANYONE WHO BRINGS YOU DOWN. IT WILL MAKE YOU FEEL BETTER, AND MEAN YOU HAVE MORE TIME TO SPEND WITH YOUR FEEL-GOOD FRIENDS!

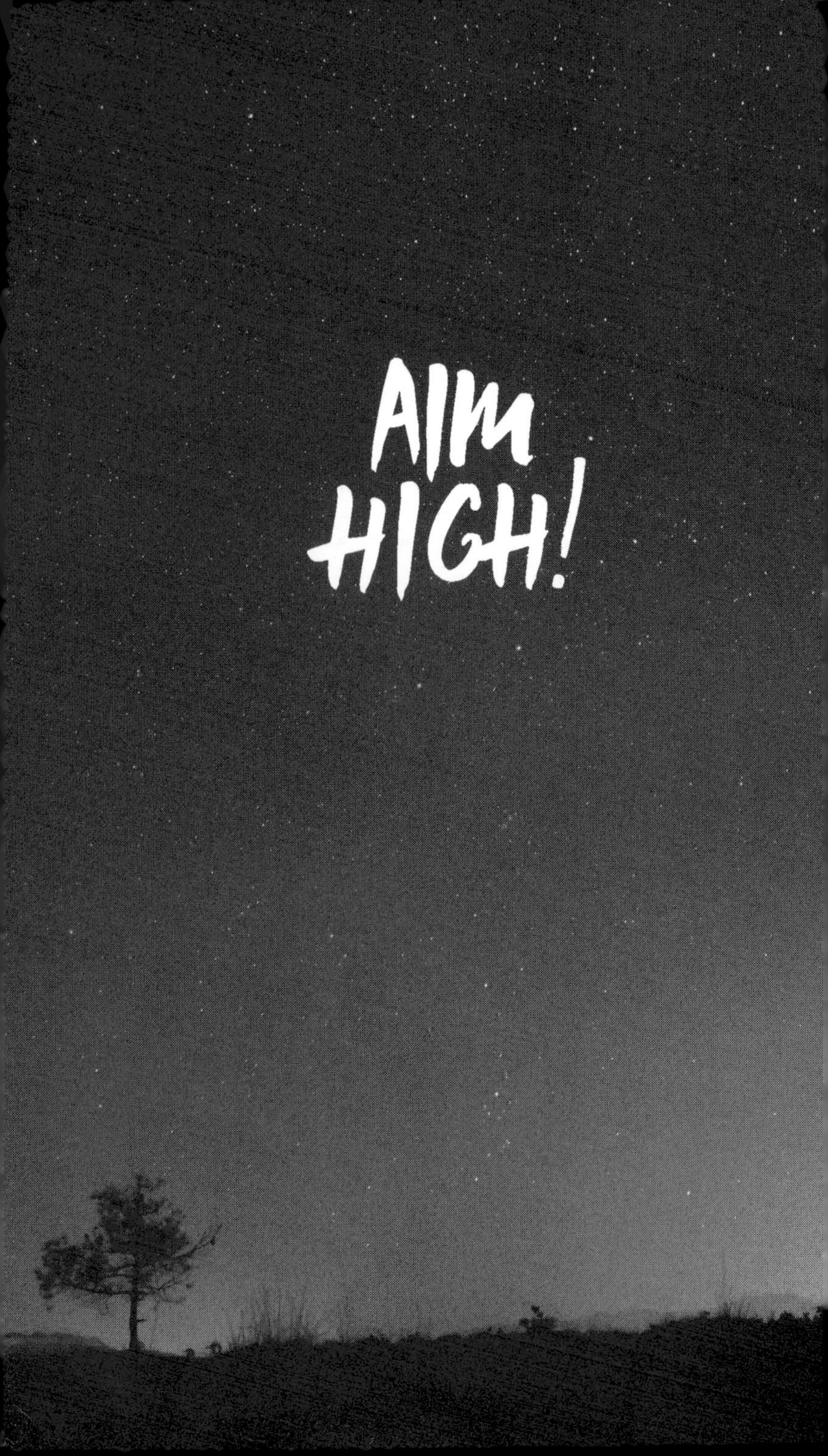
AIM
HIGH!

HAPPINESS EXERCISE 8

This meditation will help you feel more loved and supported.

1. Close your eyes, relax and imagine yourself somewhere safe and comfortable.

2. Now become aware of your breathing. Feel your body unwind with each breath, as you breathe slowly and deeply.

3. Next, picture a friendly visitor joining you. This could be someone you already know or a completely new person.

4. Imagine this visitor in as much detail as you can. How do you feel about seeing them? Do you have something to tell them? Or maybe they have a message for you?

5. Feel the visitor's love for you glowing in your heart. Their love is all around you and it feels fantastic. You deserve it.

6. Enjoy this special moment of closeness and know that next time you need reassurance, remembering these feelings will remind you of the love and support in your life.

Happiness is a direction, not a place.

"SOME PEOPLE GO TO PRIESTS, OTHERS TO POETRY. I GO TO MY FRIENDS."

VIRGINIA WOOLF

"A FRIEND IS ONE OF THE NICEST THINGS YOU CAN HAVE, AND ONE OF THE BEST THINGS YOU CAN BE."

DOUGLAS PAGELS

"FRIENDSHIP IS BORN AT THAT MOMENT WHEN ONE PERSON SAYS TO ANOTHER: 'WHAT! YOU TOO? I THOUGHT I WAS THE ONLY ONE."

C.S. LEWIS

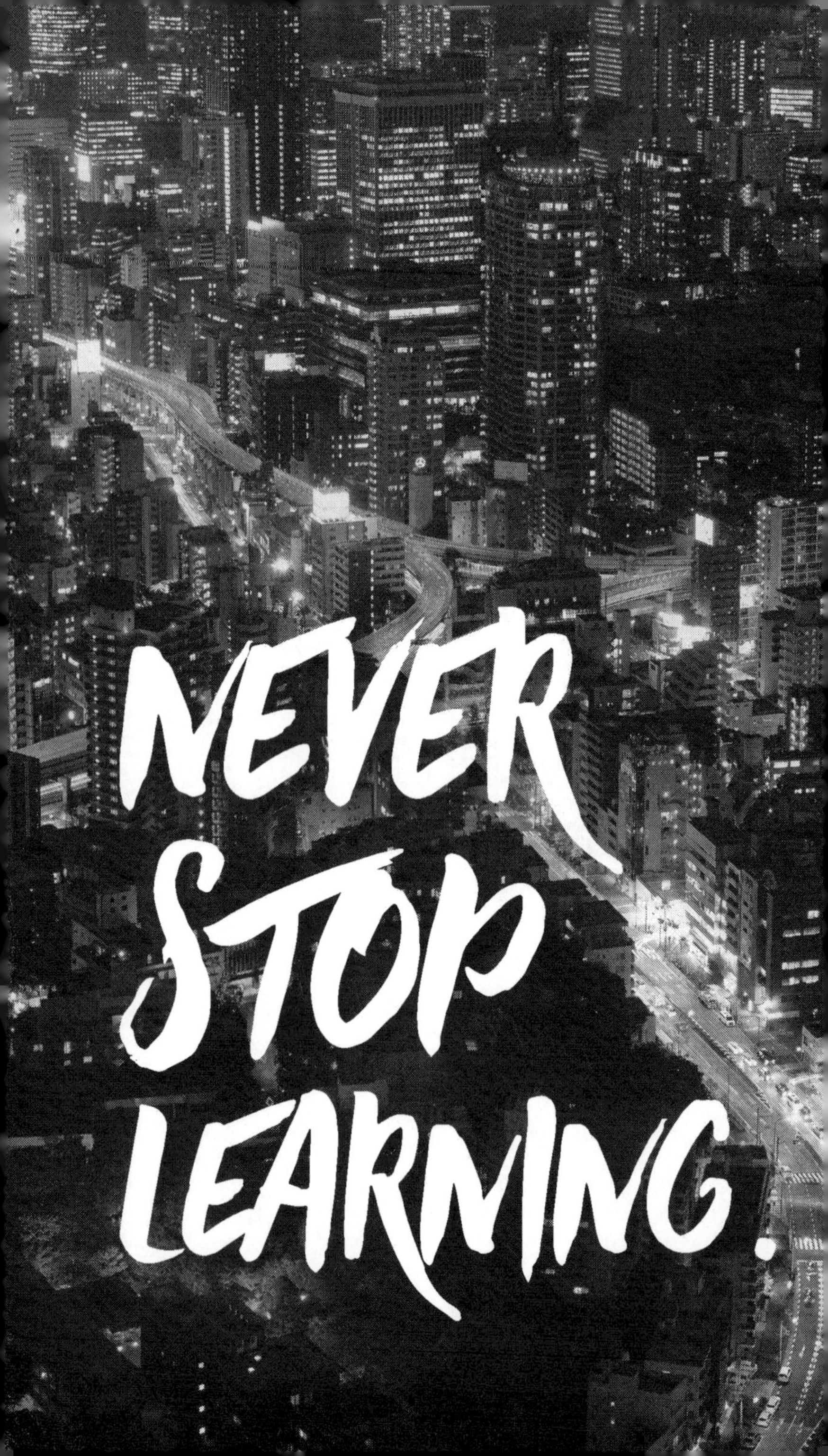
NEVER
STOP
LEARNING.

Love to learn!

Learning new things helps us feel more confident and capable, which in turn makes us feel happier. Plus, it's a great way of connecting with new people – another happiness booster!

Humans are programmed to seek out new things and reach for new heights. We all have a natural desire to learn and develop, which broadens our horizons and fuels our creativity.

Most people associate learning with a formal education and academic qualifications. However, as important as that is, it's only one type of learning.

We don't just stop developing when we leave school or university. Knowledge can be acquired and skill-sets developed just about anywhere. If you have any kind of awareness about the world, learning is pretty much unavoidable!

Having a positive attitude to personal growth and making a conscious decision to continue developing will not only make you feel more positive, it will strengthen your connection to the world, and present you with better opportunities.

So commit to becoming a life-long learner – it will improve your quality of life and have you feeling happier in no time!

Learn from yesterday.

HAPPINESS EXERCISE 9

Embrace your potential with these powerful affirmations. Just repeat them 20 times a day!

* I AM A WORK IN PROGRESS. I BELIEVE IN MYSELF AND MY ABILITIES.

* I WELCOME NEW CHANCES TO LEARN.

* I NOW RELEASE OLD HABITS AND EMBRACE THE FUTURE!

* I LEARN EXCITING LESSONS AND EXPAND MY AWARENESS EVERY DAY.

TOP TIP

Follow these simple rules to write your own affirmations...
1. Make them short so they are easier to remember.
2. Be sure to start your affirmations with 'I' or 'My'.
3. Write them in the present tense.

Your life is limitless.

"LIVE AS IF YOU WERE TO DIE TOMORROW.
LEARN AS IF YOU WERE TO LIVE FOREVER."

MAHATMA GANDHI

"LEARNING IS A TREASURE THAT WILL
FOLLOW ITS OWNER EVERYWHERE."

CHINESE PROVERB

"THE BEAUTIFUL THING ABOUT LEARNING IS
THAT NOBODY CAN TAKE IT AWAY FROM YOU."

B.B. KING

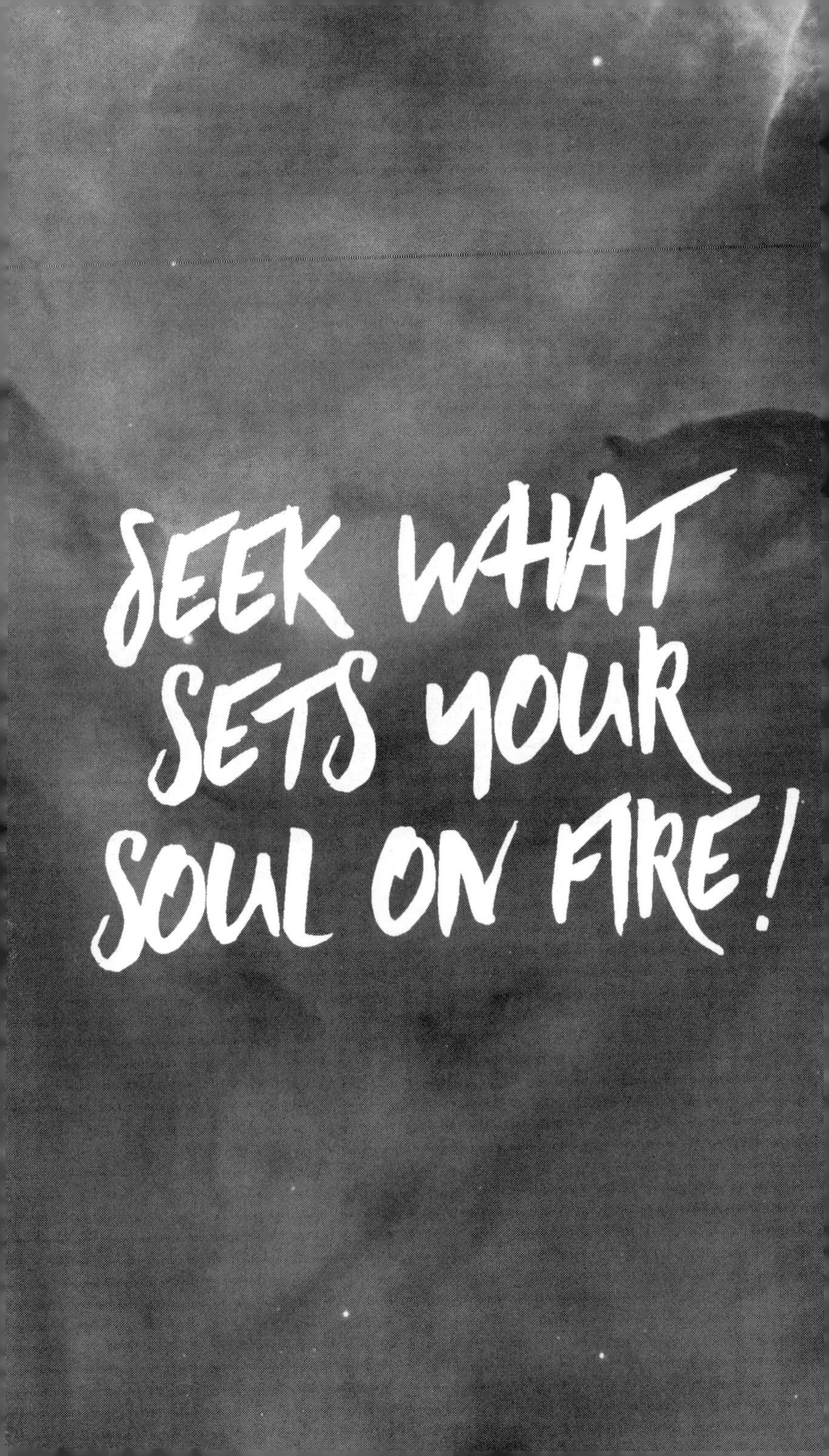
SEEK WHAT
SETS YOUR
SOUL ON FIRE!

HAPPINESS EXERCISE 10

This last Happiness Exercise is tons of fun! It's a list of 30 simple ways to introduce more happiness into your life. Try doing one thing on the list every day for a month to see which suggestions make you feel happiest!

1. GO FOR A WALK
2. WRITE A POEM
3. HELP SOMEONE
4. LISTEN TO MUSIC
5. ENJOY NATURE
6. LIST YOUR LOVES
7. WATCH A NEW FILM
8. TAKE A NAP
9. FILL IN A JOURNAL
10. TREAT YOURSELF
11. LAUGH WITH A FRIEND

things will
work out.

12 READ A BOOK
13 DANCE WILDLY!
14 MEDITATE
15 SEE FRIENDS
16 GET ARTY
17 FINISH A LIST
18 PAMPER YOURSELF
19 COOK A MEAL
20 GET DOODLING
21 LISTEN TO WATER
22 GO FOR A WORK OUT
23 BE THANKFUL
24 PLAN A FUN TRIP
25 LOVE AN ANIMAL
26 GET CUDDLY
27 DO YOGA
28 GO FOR A JOG
29 SOAK IN A BATH
30 KNOW THAT YOU
ARE LOVED

You already have it all.

ENJOY YOUR JOURNEY!

I've loved writing *How To Be Unicorn Happy* for you. I really hope you enjoy trying the ideas and suggestions in it – and that they help make you feel happier and more positive.

One thing that's become clear as I've worked on this book is that happiness isn't a destination. We need to aim for happiness every day. Work at being happier, and you'll soon start welcoming more joy into your life.

I can't promise your journey to a happier life will always be easy, but I do know it'll be worth it! I speak from experience – the techniques in this book really have helped transform my life into a much happier place.

Thank you so much for sharing this journey with me, and for supporting my work. YOU are one of the reasons my life is so full of joy and happiness, and I am so grateful!

I'D LOVE TO HEAR HOW YOU GET ON WITH THE IDEAS IN THIS BOOK! PLEASE SEND YOUR STORIES TO ME AT HAPPY@VINCENTX2.COM THANK YOU!

✳ Never forget that you are a unicorn! You deserve to live a happy life filled with only good things. Good luck!

25922521R00065

Printed in Poland
by Amazon Fulfillment
Poland Sp. z o.o., Wrocław